GOD'S LITTLE BOOK
OF PROVERBS
Timeless Wisdom for
Daily Living

Honor Books
Tulsa, Oklahoma

4th Printing

God's Little Book of Proverbs:
Timeless Wisdom for Daily Living
ISBN 1-56292-544-X
Copyright © 1999 by Honor Books
P.O. Box 55388
Tulsa, Oklahoma 74155

INTRODUCTION

Proverbs have been described as general truths based on wide experiences which demonstrate rules for living. In other words, there are universal laws that, if followed, will bring success and blessing. The Bible calls these laws, which can be found in the Book of Proverbs, the practice of wisdom.

At the same time, individuals and whole cultures may arrive at similar conclusions to the renowned Book of Proverbs. The true test of a good proverb is whether its wisdom has stood the test of time and whether it speaks a truth that is universal. God's proverbs will always lead you on the path of wisdom. It's pleasantly surprising that people over the history of time and past civilizations have arrived at many of the same conclusions. Most of humanity recognizes God's universal laws for success in life.

In *God's Little Book of Proverbs*, we at Honor Books offer you the best of man's insights and God's ultimate wisdom. As you read these truths, we hope they will enrich your life as you apply them to your daily challenges!

All hard work brings a profit, but mere talk leads only to poverty.

Proverbs 14:23

The work praises the man.

Irish Proverb

A word to the wise . . .

Make your work fun! There's nothing like the feeling of satisfaction that comes after doing your best on a project. Challenge yourself to climb to new heights. Answer the phone with a smile in your voice. Write a dynamic report. Compete with yourself to do a better job. Then notice how much more energy you have at the end of the day.

*Take away the dross
from silver,
And it will go to
the silversmith
for jewelry.*

Proverbs 25:4 NKJV

A gem cannot be
polished without
friction, nor
man perfected
without trials.

Chinese Proverb

Have you ever heard that old adage, "When life throws you a lemon, make lemonade?" We may not be able to control the circumstances around us, but we can choose our attitude. Happiness is a choice. So spin that straw into gold! Choose to rise above your trials and view your challenges in light of God's promises.

It's the wise thing to do!

Pride goes before destruction, a haughty spirit before a fall.

Proverbs 16:18

Pride is the author of every sin.

Irish Proverb

A word to the wise . . .

"Cream always rises to the top, but vinegar will curdle the milk." This was the way an older generation explained that cream—that quality of humility and sweetness in a person—would always find promotion. Rise to the top of your situation in life by treating others with kindness. Be the sweet cream in your relationships!

A lying tongue hates those who are crushed by it, And a flattering mouth works ruin.

Proverbs 26:28 NKJV

One falsehood spoils a thousand truths.

Ashanti Proverb

No matter what the situation, it's always easier to tell the truth. Did you make a mistake at work? Everyone makes mistakes; it's human nature. Truth is a fresh wind that blows away the storm clouds. Taking responsibility for your actions is satisfying and good for the soul. So the next time you're confronted with a difficult situation, tell the truth.

It's the wise thing to do!

*Do not love sleep or
you will grow poor;
stay awake and
you will have
food to spare.*

Proverbs 20:13

A sleeping cat cannot catch a rat.

Indian Proverb

A word to the wise . . .

When the alarm goes off tomorrow morning, don't hit the snooze bar. Start your day off a half hour earlier. Remember that old proverb, "The early bird catches the worm?" Smile up at the ceiling and rejoice in your new day of adventure. Life is full of possibilities. Change is possible. Remember, this is the first day of the rest of your life!

He who leans on, trusts in, and is confident of his own mind and heart is a [self-confident] fool, but he who walks in skillful and godly Wisdom shall be delivered.

Proverbs 28:26 AMP

A wise man never knows all; only a fool knows everything.

African Proverb

One of the greatest pleasures in life is discovery. What a dull world it would be if we all knew everything there was to know! All of us are ignorant, only in different ways and in different areas of knowledge. It keeps us humble. The next time you're tempted to boast of your accomplishments, remember to thank God for all He's given you.

It's the wise thing to do!

A wife of noble character who can find? She is worth far more than rubies.

Proverbs 31:10

Modesty is the beauty of women.

Gaelic Proverb

A word to the wise . . .

There's an old saying in America: "Pretty is as pretty does." Instead of aspiring to look like a fashion model, how much more attractive is a woman who is gracious, unpretentious, and who always finds a way to make you feel important. Look beyond a woman's face and find the real person. Is her beauty only skin deep, or is she a woman of substance?

The sluggard buries his hand in the dish; He is weary of bringing it to his mouth again.

Proverbs 26:15 NAS

Man who waits for roast duck to fly into mouth must wait very, very long time.

Chinese Proverb

Research has shown that people who look forward to their day are far happier than those who have no purpose in life. Goal-oriented people have more energy, stamina, and a tendency to be healthier. Remember, God gave Adam work in the Garden of Eden; he looked after the plants and animals. Work is a blessing! So the next time you sit down to eat, bless the Lord and enjoy the fruits of your labor.

It's the wise thing to do!

*As in water
face reflects face,
So a man's heart
reveals the man.*

Proverbs 27:19 NKJV

A person consists of
his faith. Whatever
is his faith,
even so is he.

Indian Proverb

A word to the wise . . .

It is said, "Whatever we feed on, that is what we become." Our minds are somewhat like sophisticated computers that retain what we see, read, and hear. Feed your spirit with uplifting, inspirational thoughts, and you'll walk with a spring in your step. Feast on love and joy, and you'll speak words of encouragement. Drink from the fountain of God's living water and you'll experience a refreshing of your soul.

A true friend is always loyal, and a brother is born to help in time of need.

Proverbs 17:17 TLB

Be honorable yourself if you wish to associate with honorable people.

Welsh Proverb

Do you remember the Golden Rule: Do unto others what you would have them do unto you? That wisdom is never more true than when applied to the people with whom you associate. If you want a true friend, be a friend who can be trusted. If you want an honorable business partner, be a person of honor. All of us desire companions who will treat us with respect.

It's the wise thing to do!

The tongue of the wise commends knowledge, but the mouth of the fool gushes folly.

Proverbs 15:2

Speak little and to the purpose.

American Proverb

A word to the wise . . .

There's an old expression that says, "He [or she] babbles like a brook." It refers to someone who talks incessantly but never says anything important. The cowboy heroes of yesteryear were always the strong, silent type, and when they talked, everyone listened. We knew what they had to say would be important. When you talk, are people tuning you out, or turning up the volume?

Wisdom and good judgment live together, for wisdom knows where to discover knowledge and understanding.

Proverbs 8:12 TLB

Call on God, but row away from the rocks.

Indian Proverb

Have you ever heard the expression, "He [or she] doesn't have the sense God gave a goose?" It's talking about someone who doesn't use any common sense. God expects us to call on him in times of need, but He also expects us to use wisdom to avoid trouble. Instead of waiting three months to balance your checkbook, tackle that task right after you receive your monthly statement.

It's the wise thing to do!

*Before his downfall
a man's heart is
proud, but humility
comes before honor.*

Proverbs 18:12

Neither praise nor blame yourself.

American Proverb

A word to the wise . . .

"Don't blow your own horn," an old maxim cautions. There's good reason for it. Boasting only creates resentment. Instead, allow others to praise you for a job well done. Do a job to the best of your ability because it's pleasing to God. He'll make sure you get promoted. Put your best foot forward, and people will notice!

The rich rule over the poor, and the borrower is servant to the lender.

Proverbs 22:7

Before you borrow money from a friend, decide which you need more.

American Proverb

There's an old American saying that advises, "Never borrow money from friends or relatives. You'll always regret it." The reason? It changes your relationship to one of borrower and lender. Friendship and family relationships are much too precious to endanger. If you want to help someone you love, consider giving them money as a gift, or not giving it at all.

It's the wise thing to do!

*The rich and
the poor have
this in common,
The Lord is the
maker of them all.*

Proverbs 22:2 NKJV

When the sun rises, it rises for everyone.

Cuban Proverb

A word to the wise . . .

God is no respecter of persons. He sends rain to water the daisies as well as the roses. Some may have more wealth than others, but God looks at the character of our hearts. We are His children, and if we ask, He will answer our prayers. Have you asked for help today? Seek God for opportunity and watch Him open new vistas for you!

Be with wise men
and become wise.
Be with evil men
and become evil.

Proverbs 13:20 TLB

He who walks with
the lame learns
how to limp.

Latin Proverb

Often we fall into relationships with people without much thought about how their company affects us. But the fact is, our friends often have more influence over our actions than our families. If you desire more wisdom and knowledge, make friends with someone who will challenge you to step up to the mark of excellence. Find a mentor.

It's the wise thing to do!

Timely advice is as lovely as golden apples in a silver basket.

Proverbs 25:11 TLB

Only your real friends will tell you when your face is dirty.

Sicilian Proverb

A word to the wise . . .

We've all been there. Sometime in the afternoon, you look in the mirror only to discover a piece of lettuce stuck in your teeth or a mustard smudge on your face. You've talked to several people since lunch, but no one has bothered to tell you about it. True friends will prevent you from embarrassing yourself. Do you have a close friend who loves you enough to tell you the truth?

Sometimes mere
words are not
enough—discipline
is needed.

Proverbs 29:19 TLB

After all is said
and done, more is
said than done.

American Proverb

"Stop yakking and get cracking," says one old adage. In offices all around the world, there are people who never seem to get anything done because of their incessant talking. Most of them are complaining about all the work they have to do! The next time you're tempted to gripe about your workload, take the same amount of time you would have spent sounding off and prioritize your projects.

It's the wise thing to do!

A man has joy by the answer of his mouth, And a word spoken in due season, how good it is!

Proverbs 15:23 NKJV

A good word costs
no more than
a bad one.

English Proverb

A word to the wise . . .

There's an old proverb that says, "You can catch more flies with honey than vinegar." A smile is quick to deliver and makes us feel as good as the person who receives it. Why then don't we smile more often? How much more productive it is to compliment a person than to deliver criticism. Smile the next time you think the checker at the grocery store is too slow, and watch it change your attitude.

*Hope deferred
makes the heart
sick, but a longing
fulfilled is
a tree of life.*

Proverbs 13:12

More people fail
for lack of
encouragement
than for any
other reason.

American Proverb

There are a great many talented and gifted people throughout the world who never fulfill all that God has planned for them. It isn't a lack of knowledge that holds them back. More often it's because no one has bothered to pat them on the back and cheer them on. Is there someone around you who lacks the confidence to succeed? Encourage them to go for it!

It's the wise thing to do . . .

The man of few words and settled mind is wise; therefore, even a fool is thought to be wise when he is silent. It pays him to keep his mouth shut.

Proverbs 17:27-28
TLB

He who knows little knows enough if he knows how to hold his tongue.

Italian Proverb

A word to the wise . . .

Silence is golden, especially when you don't know what you're talking about. Many people think they can bluff and double-talk their way through life. But a fool sticks out like a sore thumb. People who hold their tongues and learn to listen appear far wiser, and through the art of listening, wisdom is soon gained.

A wise youth makes hay while the sun shines, but what a shame to see a lad who sleeps away his hour of opportunity.

Proverbs 10:5 TLB

The lazier a man is, the more he plans to do tomorrow.

Norwegian Proverb

Many a person has said, "I'll do it tomorrow." But by tomorrow, the task is forgotten. The minutes add up to hours, and hours into days, and days into years. "Don't put off until tomorrow what can be done today, for tomorrow may never come," advises one wise saying. Have you been putting off something you should have tackled long ago? Go ahead and get it over with.

———◦❋◦———

It's the wise thing to do!

The appetite of the
laborer works for
him, for
[the need of]
his mouth
urges him on.

Proverbs 16:26 AMP

When one must,
one can. For it
is by hunger.

Yiddish Proverb

A word to the wise . . .

Most of us work because we have to feed ourselves and our families. That's a good thing! There's nothing wrong with being motivated by fulfillment of a basic need. God intended that we should work. Since we have the privilege of working, then we might as well enjoy it! If you don't like your present job, then look until you find that one special place where you belong.

Any story sounds true until someone tells the other side and sets the record straight.

Proverbs 18:17 TLB

A wise man hears one word and understands two. There are two sides to every story.

Yiddish Proverb

Experience teaches us to "read between the lines." It's easy to take one person's side over another before you hear the whole story. We've all done it. But most disagreements are caused by a lack of communication—two-way communication. Until you know what really happened, refrain from forming any judgments or making any major decisions about someone's future.

———⟫•⟪———

It's the wise thing to do!

*Gossip separates
the best of friends.*

Proverbs 16:28 TLB

Whoever gossips to
you will gossip
about you.

Spanish Proverb

A word to the wise . . .

"Never turn your back on a snake," the old-timers say. Knowing the latest rumors about a person or situation gives some people a feeling of importance. So if someone is constantly telling you tales about other friends, beware. Chances are when you're not around, that person is spreading your secrets to others. Know where to draw the line with certain friends. Trust must be earned.

*My son, if
sinners entice you,
Do not consent.*

Proverbs 1:10 NKJV

Good habits result
from resisting
temptation.

Ancient Proverb

It's easier to swim downstream than battle the current. Most people float through life, and seldom resist the temptation "to have their cake and eat it too." But good habits result from a conscious decision to do the right thing, no matter how hard, whether it's pushing back from the table when we've had enough to eat, or holding our temper when provoked. Decide on a new habit you'd like to form, and practice it for the next twenty-one days.

It's the wise thing to do!

A cheerful look brings joy to the heart, and good news gives health to the bones.

Proverbs 15:30

The "small change" of human happiness lies in the unexpected friendly word.

American Proverb

A word to the wise . . .

Do you need a word of encouragement?
The word gospel means good news.
Instead of "looking for love in all the
wrong places," open your Bible today and
read God's promise to "never leave you
nor forsake you." The Word of God can
mend a broken heart and offer
hope to the hopeless.

Who can say, "I have made my heart clean, I am pure from sin"?

Proverbs 20:9 NKJV

Wink at small faults, for you have great ones yourself.

Scottish Proverb

One famous Scripture advises us to ignore the splinter in our brother's eye until we remove the log from our own. It's easy to point a finger at someone else's fault, but it's quite different when someone draws attention to our own. All of us have shortcomings, so maybe we should work on our own issues before trying to fix the rest of the world.

It's the wise thing to do!

Let another praise you, and not your own mouth; a stranger, and not your own lips.

Proverbs 27:2 RSV

When deeds speak, words are nothing.

African Proverb

A word to the wise . . .

"Deeds speak louder than words," one proverb says. So instead of boasting about your skills, it's better to let someone else spread the word about your commitment to excellence. Think about it. If you receive great service at a restaurant, don't you recommend it to your friends? The same is true of good character. People always remember a kind word and special attention.

*The Lord detests
lying lips, but he
delights in men
who are truthful.*

Proverbs 12:22

A half truth is
a whole lie.

Yiddish Proverb

It's challenging in the workplace today to maintain our integrity. But it can be done if we purpose in our hearts never to tell a lie . . . not even a "white lie." Many administrative assistants have been asked by their bosses to say they're not in. How about telling your customers your boss is "unavailable." It's the truth, and everyone wins!

⟶⟩●⟨⟵

It's the wise thing to do!

A man of
understanding
has wisdom.

Proverbs 10:23 NKJV

Some men go
through a forest
and see no
firewood.

English Proverb

A word to the wise . . .

Opportunities are all around us. But sometimes we get so focused on the task at hand that "we can't see the forest for the trees." Take time to pull back and assess your circumstances. Dream. Observe. Plan. By looking at your life from a different viewpoint, you gain knowledge and understanding. Then you can implement your goals with wisdom.

*Some men are so
lazy they won't even
feed themselves!*

Proverbs 19:24 TLB

God gives the nuts,
but he does not
crack them.

German Proverb

When God brings opportunity, He expects you to make the most of it. Tell yourself that failure is not an option. It takes perseverance to fill your bag with nuts, crack and shell them, and then bake a batch of cookies. Is there an easier way? Most likely. Look for new ideas and inventions to streamline your work. Work smarter!

It's the wise thing to do!

A fortune made by a lying tongue is a fleeting vapor and a deadly snare.

Proverbs 21:6

Ill-gotten gains never prosper.

French Proverb

A word to the wise . . .

There's a commercial that depicts sharks swimming on Wall Street as if that were the only way to prosper. But the world is full of millionaires who amassed their fortunes with honesty and integrity. They not only support their communities by supplying jobs, but they also give to worthy charities because it gives them great satisfaction. If your goal is to make a fortune, do it God's way!

The righteous care about justice for the poor, but the wicked have no such concern.

Proverbs 29:7

The rich break the law and the poor are punished for it.

Spanish Proverb

Good men and women, whether rich, middle-class, or poor, care about others. They give of their time, talent, and money to help those less fortunate than they. Many who were once homeless now serve hot meals to those who still live on the streets. We can all do something to improve the circumstances of others. Have you volunteered lately?

———➣●⬤⬤———

It's the wise thing to do!

The way of a fool seems right to him, but a wise man listens to advice.

Proverbs 12:15

He who asks is a fool for five minutes. He who does not ask remains a fool forever.

Chinese Proverb

A word to the wise . . .

We've all been in new situations. Perhaps we move to a new city or start a new job. There's that awkward period when we all have to ask questions. Better to appear foolish for a short time than to stumble in the dark forever. A wise person asks questions. Before you know it, you'll be an "old hand" and can make someone else's transition smoother. Reach out to someone who needs your help.

Better is a little with righteousness than great revenues without right.

Proverbs 16:8 KJV

Success is not defined by obtaining everything you want, but by appreciating everything you have.

Chinese Proverb

Despite the bumper sticker that says, "He who dies with the most toys wins," success in life is not about acquiring the most possessions. It's about being thankful for what you have. A grateful heart receives each new blessing in life as if it were a gift from heaven. Indeed, it is! As the old hymn says, "Thank God from Whom all blessings flow."

It's the wise thing to do!

Let not loyalty and faithfulness forsake you; bind them about your neck, write them on the tablet of your heart.

Proverbs 3:3 RSV

Dedication is not what others expect of you, it is what you can give to others.

American Proverb

A word to the wise . . .

Most happy and successful people start out serving others, no matter what their profession. Loyalty to an employer is rewarded by promotion. Faithfulness to a spouse is rewarded by a harmonious home life. Dedication to God helps us to walk a straight line through the circumstances of life. Even if you're working at a fast-food restaurant, make the best burger you can and serve it with a smile.

Take heed to the path of your feet, then all your ways will be sure. Do not swerve to the right or to the left; turn your foot away from evil.

Proverbs 4:26-27 RSV

Nobody trips over mountains. It is the small pebble that causes you to stumble. Pass all the pebbles in your path, and you will find that you have crossed the mountain.

Anonymous Proverb

Sometimes we're so eager to climb the mountains before us that we forget to keep an eye on the rocks that could trip us up. Wisdom tells us we not only need long-term goals, but we also need to pay attention to how we get to the top. Then we can enjoy the victory without having to bandage the broken toes of our companions. Remember to treat others as you would have them treat you.

⟶⟶⟶≫◦≪⟵⟵⟵

It's the wise thing to do!

*A good name is
rather to be chosen
than great riches,
and loving favor
rather than
silver and gold.*

Proverbs 22:1 AMP

Life is for one
generation; a good
name is forever.

Japanese Proverb

A word to the wise . . .

Most everyone is proud of their family name. They regale you with stories of long-ago Indian maidens, Scottish clansmen, or African kings. We're proud of our ancestors' brave deeds and courageous journeys. What kind of legacy will we pass on to the generations after us? Will they speak lovingly of us and tell of our honor? Treasure your name as if it were gold. You are worth far more to a loving God.

He who gathers in
summer is a wise
son; He who sleeps
in harvest is a son
who causes shame.

Proverbs 10:5 NKJV

It is later than you think.

Chinese Proverb

When we're young, we think we will live forever! We venture down unknown roads, and if we reach a dead-end, we merely go back to the beginning and search for another path. Yet God expects even young people to act with wisdom. Life is but a breath, Scripture says, and we are to make the most of it while we're here. Explore the paths that God sets before you.

It's the wise thing to do!

He who walks
uprightly walks
securely, but he who
takes a crooked way
shall be found out
and punished.

Proverbs 10:9 AMP

If you don't want anyone to know it, don't do it.

Chinese Proverb

A word to the wise . . .

Scripture says to shun even the "appearance" of evil. There's a reason for this. If you always walk circumspectly, never giving anyone cause to question your motives, you'll never have to retrace your steps or explain yourself. But those deeds done in secret will always come to the light of day. So make it a practice to live your life as though you were living it on a stage before the whole world.

*Correct your son,
and he will give you
rest; yes, he will give
delight to your heart.*

Proverbs 29:17 AMP

Govern a small
family as you
would cook a small
fish—very gently.

Chinese Proverb

If you've ever grilled a fish over hot coals,
you know that it must be handled gently.
If the fire is too hot it will burn the fish, or
if the fish is overcooked it will flake apart
and fall into the flames. Children are just
as tender and should be treated with great
care. Discipline them with a firm hand and
a loving, compassionate heart—
never in "red-hot" anger.

———◦∙◦———

It's the wise thing to do!

He who heeds discipline shows the way to life, but whoever ignores correction leads others astray.

Proverbs 10:17

He who lives without discipline dies without honor.

Icelandic Proverb

A word to the wise . . .

Without discipline, an army would run at the first shots of the enemy. But soldiers are trained to work as a unit, sticking shoulder-to-shoulder in the trenches. If discipline is lovingly applied to children, they will grow into disciplined adults who fulfill their commitments and stick to a task until it's finished, even when life is exploding all around them. Adopt the "buddy system" and help a friend through life.

He who guards his mouth and his tongue keeps himself from troubles.

Proverbs 21:23 AMP

While the word is yet unspoken, you are master of it; when once it is spoken, it is master of you.

Arabian Proverb

"Think before you speak," a wise saying goes. Have you ever said something, and the instant it was out of your mouth, you wanted to snatch it back? We all have. After all, we're human. An apt Scripture reminds us to "Fix your thoughts on what is true and good and right." (Philippians 4:8 TLB). If we do, we'll always speak words of life!

It's the wise thing to do!

*He who answers
a matter before
he hears it,
It is folly and
shame to him.*

Proverbs 18:13 *NKJV*

Only judge when you have heard all.

Greek Proverb

A word to the wise . . .

Most people have a desire to do what's right. But our world is moving at such a fast pace, sometimes we don't take the time to gather all the facts before we rush to judgment— whether at home, in a social setting, or in the business world. The next time you're asked to make a decision, instead of "shooting from the hip," take a deep breath and listen to the whole story before you act.

Dishonest money dwindles away, but he who gathers money little by little makes it grow.

Proverbs 13:11

What comes with ease, goes with ease.

Arabian Proverb

"A penny saved is a penny earned," is an old maxim handed down through the generations. Accounting teachers frequently ask their students whether they would rather have $10,000 in one lump sum, or a penny doubled every day. Which is more valuable? A penny doubled daily is a simple lesson in the value of compound interest. At the end of a month, it would yield a fortune! Start a savings account today and watch it grow.

⋘⋙

It's the wise thing to do!

*The good man's
earnings advance
the cause of
righteousness.
The evil man
squanders his
on sin.*

Proverbs 10:16 TLB

What's got badly, goes badly.

Irish Proverb

A word to the wise . . .

Have you ever heard someone say, "Easy come, easy go?" It's usually the rationale gamblers use when they win big, place another bet, and then lose everything. The race between the tortoise and the hare illustrates the principle that "slow and steady wins the race." What kind of money manager are you? Purpose to spend your money in a way that's pleasing to God.

With patience a ruler may be persuaded, and a soft tongue will break a bone.

Proverbs 25:15 RSV

The less sound a man's argument, the louder he talks.

American Proverb

President Teddy Roosevelt once said, "Walk softly and carry a big stick." His philosophy of diplomacy was one of persuasion coupled with power. So when everyone else is shouting their ideas, speak softly, and your whisper will be heard if you back it up with solid reasoning and innovative suggestions. Jesus spoke to the storm in Mark 4:39 (KJV) and said, "Peace, be still!" It worked! Why not give it a try?

It's the wise thing to do!

*Truth stands the
test of time;
lies are soon
exposed.*

Proverbs 12:19 TLB

To tell a lie might
help you to have
lunch, but not
to have supper.

Arabian Proverb

A word to the wise . . .

"There's no such thing as a free lunch," someone has said. It's true. When something sounds too good to be true, it usually is. There's a catch somewhere—a lie—hidden in the small print. That's why it's always sensible to read a contract carefully and make sure you can live with its long-term consequences. Scripture says in John 8:32, "You will know the truth, and the truth will set you free."

A fool finds no pleasure in understanding but delights in airing his own opinions.

Proverbs 18:2

Never argue with a fool. Someone watching may not be able to tell the difference.

Anonymous Proverb

Someone once said, "Suffer not a fool."
So the next time someone makes an
outrageous remark in your presence, walk
away. Life is too short to engage a fool in
an argument. Your time is much too
valuable! Instead, read a motivational or
inspirational book, write a letter, or set
your goals for the year. It's amazing
how much more time you'll have.

———≈⊃●⊂≈———

It's the wise thing to do!

Lazy men are soon poor; hard workers get rich.

Proverbs 10:4 TLB

God says, "Rise and I shall rise with you." He does not say, "Sleep and I shall feed you."

Arabian Proverb

A word to the wise . . .

There's a middle road to walk between being lazy and becoming a workaholic. The lazy man expects someone else to feed him. The workaholic depends only on himself. The truth is, God has said we are not to worry about what we shall eat or drink. But our faith doesn't relieve us of our responsibilities. In the morning when you wake, rejoice in a new day full of God's mercies and opportunities!

A man who isolates himself seeks his own desire; He rages against all wise judgment.

Proverbs 18:1 NKJV

Loneliness
breaks the spirit.

Jewish Proverb

Studies have shown that people who have many friends live longer than those who isolate themselves from others. Man is a social being. You don't have to be lonely. The next time you find yourself feeling alone, visit a nursing home or a homeless shelter. Take a treat to an elderly neighbor. Volunteer at a local hospital.

It's the wise thing to do!

For a righteous man falls seven times and rises again, but the wicked are overthrown by calamity.

Proverbs 24:16 AMP

Fall seven times; stand up eight.

Japanese Proverb

A word to the wise . . .

Despite the fact that he only had three months of formal schooling and suffered progressive hearing loss, Thomas Edison invented the incandescent light bulb, microphone, record player, and motion picture. His inventions failed hundreds of times until he found just the right combination of materials. What made him so successful? Every time he fell down, he got right back up again.

There are those who [generously] scatter abroad, and yet increase more; there are those who withhold more than is fitting or what is justly due, but it results only in want.

Proverbs 11:24 AMP

What I kept, I lost; what I spent, I had; what I gave, I have.

Persian Proverb

"It is more blessed to give than to receive" (Acts 20:35 KJV). Our parents have taught us this Scriptural principle since we were children. Curious as it may seem, when you give away your love, your time, or your treasure, you end up with far more than you lose. Just as a farmer scatters seeds and receives a bountiful crop, so our gifts are multiplied into the lives of others. Give the gift of yourself, and watch your spirit grow!

It's the wise thing to do!

*I love those
who love me,
And those who seek
me diligently will
find me.*

Proverbs 8:17 NKJV

Weave in faith and God will find the thread.

Anonymous Proverb

A word to the wise . . .

When we look at the tapestry of our lives from this side of eternity, it often appears to be nothing more than unconnected, colorful threads. Yet from God's side, you are weaving a portrait of your life. Place your life in God's hands, and the Master Weaver will disentangle all those loose strands and make sense of your dropped stitches. Today, ask Him to take over the fabrication of your life!

The father of the righteous will greatly rejoice; he who begets a wise son will be glad in him.

Proverbs 23:24 RSV

A father who teaches his children responsibility provides them with a fortune.

Anonymous Proverb

Have you ever heard the phrase, "Do as I say, not as I do?" It doesn't work. Children are little sponges who soak up every word or deed of ours. If you want your child to be responsible, vote in every election. If you want her to be dependable, pick her up at school on time. If you want him to be generous, give to the Salvation Army or some other worthy charity.

It's the wise thing to do!

How long will you lie there, you sluggard? When will you get up from your sleep?

Proverbs 6:9

A man grows most tired while standing still.

Chinese Proverb

A word to the wise . . .

There's nothing more tiring than doing nothing. Exercise is invigorating! Do you need to battle the bulge? Take a brisk walk during lunch. Don't wait for someone else to start first. Step out as a leader and watch others fall in behind you. Everyone else is waiting for an incentive to get moving, so organize a walking club. Then watch those extra pounds melt away.

A man's mind plans his way, but the Lord directs his steps and makes them sure.

Proverbs 16:9 AMP

Man drives, but it is God who holds the reins.

Jewish Proverbs

Have you ever seen the bumper sticker that reads, "God is my copilot?" Consider letting Him sit in the *pilot's* seat. Write down your top ten goals, asking God for His direction. Don't be surprised if He challenges you to dream big dreams! Luke 18:27 says, "What is impossible with men is possible with God."

It's the wise thing to do!

Do not withhold good from those who deserve it, when it is in your power to act.

Proverbs 3:27

He gives twice who gives quickly.

English Proverb

A word to the wise...

All of us at one time or another have thought about helping someone, only to be distracted and forget about the situation. Perhaps someone's car broke down, and that person needed a lift to work. Because no one helped out, your coworker missed a day's pay. So the next time you see someone in need, be quick to act. You'll have made a friend, and you'll have someone to ask for help when you're in need.

He who walks with the wise grows wise, but a companion of fools suffers harm.

Proverbs 13:20

When the character of a man is not clear, look at his friends.

Japanese Proverb

"You're judged by the company you keep,"
an old adage says. You may be an honest
businessman, but if you hang around
someone with a bad reputation, it will rub
off on you. People will wonder if you are
just as dishonest. Remember,
your name is worth more than gold,
so consider well those persons
with whom you do business.

It's the wise thing to do!

Acquitting the guilty and condemning the innocent—the LORD detests them both.

Proverbs 17:15

Never criticize a man until you have walked a mile in his moccasins.

American Indian Proverb

A word to the wise…

"Judge not that you be not judged," Matthew 7:1 says (NKJV). Often, we're hasty in our judgments of others. When they make mistakes, we boast that it could never happen to us. Yet we cannot know the state of that person's mind when it happened. What circumstances contributed to his or her error? The next time someone falls down, pick that person up and dust him off. Help put a spring back in his step!

Have two goals: wisdom—that is, knowing and doing right—and common sense. Don't let them slip away, for they fill you with living energy, and are a feather in your cap.

Proverbs 3:21-22 TLB

One pound of learning requires ten pounds of common sense to apply it.

Persian Proverb

"A little common sense goes a long way," an old saying goes. For instance, we may learn how an airplane engine works, but it would be dangerous to take the controls and fly it. We need to use our common sense when we're faced with unusual circumstances. James 1:5 says that if we ask for wisdom, it will be given to us liberally. The next time you're in a tough spot, use a little common sense.

It's the wise thing to do!

Choose my instruction instead of silver, knowledge rather than choice gold.

Proverbs 8:10

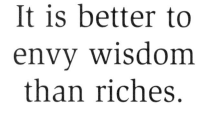

It is better to envy wisdom than riches.

Greek Proverb

A word to the wise...

When Solomon ascended to his father David's throne, rather than ask God for more riches, he asked for wisdom. Because of his request, God not only made him the wisest man in the world, but He granted Solomon riches and fame as well. Instead of praying for more money or your first big break, try asking for more insight. The payoff just may be greater!

Do not set foot on the path of the wicked or walk in the way of evil men. Avoid it, do not travel on it; turn from it and go on your way.

Proverbs 4:14-15

Opportunity may knock only once, but temptation leans on the doorbell.

American Proverb

"It's hard to stop a freight train once it's left the station," an old saying goes. In other words, once you yield to temptation, it's hard to stop and retrace your steps. The best way to avoid the pitfalls of life is through knowledge and understanding. If you know what quicksand looks like, you're not likely to step in it. Fill your mind with good thoughts, and stay on the path of victory.

It's the wise thing to do!

Ants are creatures of little strength, yet they store up their food in the summer.

Proverbs 30:25

Frugality is the sure guard of our virtues.

Indian Proverb

A word to the wise...

"Save your money for a rainy day," goes one old adage. In years gone by, thriftiness was a virtue practiced by almost everyone. Credit cards and overdraft protection did not exist. You couldn't spend more than you earned. Everyone had a summer garden and canned vegetables to take them through the winter. Are you spending more than you earn? Try setting up a monthly budget and become more aware of where you're spending your hard-earned money. You'll be glad you did!

*Instruct a wise man
and he will be
wiser still; teach
a righteous man
and he will add
to his learning.*

Proverbs 9:9

Give a man a fish, and
you feed him for a day.
Teach a man to fish, and
you feed him for a lifetime.

Japanese Proverb

America is one of the most generous nations in the world. We give money, clothes, and food to other nations. We buy candy bars from Little Leaguers and cookies from Girl Scouts. The one commodity in short supply, however, is the gift of time. Rather than teaching young people what we've learned from our experiences, we figure someone else will do it. Have you passed on your knowledge and skills yet? Become a mentor and teach someone to fish!

It's the wise thing to do!

A word aptly spoken is like apples of gold in settings of silver.

Proverbs 25:11

A word of kindness is better than a fat pie.

Russian Proverb

A word to the wise...

Have you ever heard the saying, "Kindness is catching?" Try it. The next time a waitress goes the extra mile for you, smile and say thanks. How about the teenager at the fast-food place who gives you great service? Tell him his attitude will take him far in life. Then there's the woman who holds the door open for an elderly person. Make a point to tell her someone noticed. It will make her day!

The Lord detests men of perverse heart but he delights in those whose ways are blameless.

Proverbs 11:20

You cannot drive straight on a twisting lane.

Russian Proverb

"He's a real straight arrow," is a saying often used to describe someone who is unfailingly honest. It's not easy to stand up for what's right when everyone around you is fudging on their taxes or taking home office supplies. But it can be done. So be the first in your crowd to set an example. Be a "straight arrow" for God!

It's the wise thing to do!

When pride comes, then comes disgrace; but with the humble is wisdom.

Proverbs 11:2 RSV

Temper gets you in trouble. Pride keeps you there.

Anonymous Proverb

A word to the wise...

Scripture says, "Pride goeth before destruction" (Proverbs 16:18 KJV). Why is that? Because pride believes it is always right and never listens to advice to the contrary. Unfortunately, Napoleon thought the same thing before he was defeated at Waterloo. It takes a humble person to admit when he or she is wrong. The next time you get mad, be quick to forgive or apologize. You'll sleep much better!

*Make plans by
seeking advice;
if you wage war,
obtain guidance.*

Proverbs 20:18

Vision without action is a daydream. Action without vision is a nightmare.

Japanese Proverb

"Before you get on the train, you better ask where it's going," an old saying goes. If you wanted to invest in the stock market, you would ask an expert for advice. Dreams will take you a long way, but if you need a loan, the bank will want a business plan. Wise counsel can save you a lot of heartache! So the next time you're contemplating a new enterprise, ask for guidance.

It's the wise thing to do!

*Do not be afraid
of sudden terror,
Nor of trouble from
the wicked when
it comes; for the
Lord will be
your confidence,
And will keep your
foot from
being caught.*

Proverbs 3:25-26

NKJV

Turn your face to
the sun and the
shadows fall
behind you.

Maori Proverb

A word to the wise...

"Fear not!" Scripture repeats that phrase 365 times, once for every day of the year. God loves us so much that He never wants us to be afraid. Put your trust in the Creator of the universe, the One who spread the grass as a carpet under your feet and hung the blue sky as a canopy over your head. Knowing that God is your Protector will give you great confidence to face whatever life brings!

Counsel in the heart of man is like deep water, But a man of understanding will draw it out.

Proverbs 20:5 NKJV

A real friend is one who helps us to think our noblest thoughts, put forth our best efforts, and to be our best selves.

Anonymous Proverb

"No man is an island," we have always heard. Friends are our greatest allies. Life certainly would not be the same without them. A true friend builds us up and cheers us on. Friends listen. Do your friends bring out the best in you? If not, then it's time to find new friends.

It's the wise thing to do!

Do not forsake your friend and the friend of your father, and do not go to your brother's house when disaster strikes you— better to a neighbor nearby than a brother far away.

Proverbs 27:10

The path to a friend's house is short.

Anonymous Proverb

A word to the wise...

"A friend is closer than a brother," it is sometimes said. In fact, our friends are usually *closer* to us than our families. We share our hopes and dreams with them. They know when we're in trouble. We work with them, and they are our neighbors. A good friend is more valuable than gold. Make a friend you can trust and depend upon.

*The wicked is
ensnared by
the transgression
of his lips,
But the righteous
will come
through trouble.*

Proverbs 12:13 *NKJV*

You cannot prevent the
birds of sorrow from flying
over your head, but you
can prevent them from
building nests in your hair.

Chinese Proverb

We're constantly bombarded by the media with reasons to be depressed. But how we decide to react to the challenges of life is our choice. Attitude is everything. God has promised in His Word that He's always with us and that He has sent His angels to protect us. So, as it says in Romans 8:31 (KJV), "If God be for us, who can be against us?" Turn your life over to God today!

It's the wise thing to do!

The fear of the LORD is the beginning of knowledge: but fools despise wisdom and instruction.

Proverbs 1:7 KJV

If you refuse to be made straight when you are green, you will not be made straight when you are dry.

African Proverb

A word to the wise...

"A green twig is hard to break," many of us have heard as we were growing up. When you remain flexible and pliable in the hands of God, He can mold and shape you into your ultimate best. And if you continue to be teachable, you will never grow old. Just as you did when you were a child, you will stand in wonder and awe at the mysteries of God's great universe.

Humility and the fear of the Lord bring wealth and honor and life.

Proverbs 22:4

The first test of a really great man is his humility.

American Proverb

"Humble yourselves in the sight of the Lord, and He shall lift you up," the Scripture says in James 4:10 (KJV). It is one of the great paradoxes of all time. Jesus humbled Himself on a cross so that we might be lifted up. The way to true success and honor is through humble submission to God. Try putting God and others first in your life and watch what God will do!

It's the wise thing to do!

If you are looking for advice, stay away from fools.

Proverbs 14:7 TLB

The fool has his answer on the edge of his tongue.

Arabian Proverb

A word to the wise...

It says in Psalm 32:8, "I will instruct you and teach you in the way you should go; I will counsel you and watch over you." There's no reason to seek out fools for advice. God has all the answers, and if you listen to His advice, you'll always make the right decision. The next time you're faced with two different paths, just ask yourself, *What would Jesus do?* You'll make the right choice!

Additional copies of this book
are available from your local bookstore.

Also available from the God's Little series:

God's Little Instruction Book series
God's Little Devotional Book series
God's Little Lessons on Life series

Honor Books
Tulsa, Oklahoma